First World War
and Army of Occupation
War Diary
France, Belgium and Germany

GUARDS DIVISION
1 Guards Brigade
Headquarters
1 May 1917 - 31 May 1917

WO95/1213/8

The Naval & Military Press Ltd
www.nmarchive.com
Published in association with The National Archives

Published by

The Naval & Military Press Ltd

Unit 10 Ridgewood Industrial Park,

Uckfield, East Sussex,

TN22 5QE England

Tel: +44 (0) 1825 749494

www.naval-military-press.com

www.nmarchive.com

This diary has been reprinted in facsimile from the original. Any imperfections are inevitably reproduced and the quality may fall short of modern type and cartographic standards.

© **Crown Copyright**
Images reproduced by permission of The National Archives, London, England, 2015.

Contents

Document type	Place/Title	Date From	Date To
Heading	WO95/1213 May 1917		
War Diary	Bronfay Farm Camp 15	01/05/1917	05/05/1917
War Diary	Bronfay Farm Camp 15	03/05/1917	09/05/1917
War Diary	Bronfay Fm To Le-Mesnil-En-Arrouaise	10/05/1917	12/05/1917
War Diary	Le Mesnil En-Arrouaise	12/05/1917	18/05/1917
War Diary	Le Mesnil To Bronfay Camp 15	20/05/1917	20/05/1917
War Diary	Bronfay Camp 15 to Sailly Laurette	21/05/1917	21/05/1917
War Diary	Sailly Laurette	22/05/1917	31/05/1917
War Diary		28/05/1917	31/05/1917
War Diary	Renescure	30/05/1917	31/05/1917
Miscellaneous	1st Guards Brigade Platoon Competition.		
Operation(al) Order(s)	1st Guards Brigade Order No. 122.	07/05/1917	07/05/1917
Miscellaneous	March Table.		
Miscellaneous	Warning Order.	15/05/1917	15/05/1917
Operation(al) Order(s)	1st Guards Brigade Order No. 123.	18/05/1917	18/05/1917
Miscellaneous	March Table.		
Miscellaneous	Distribution Of 1st Guards Brigade On May 21st.	21/05/1917	21/05/1917
Operation(al) Order(s)	1st Guards Brigade Order No. 124.	28/05/1917	28/05/1917
Miscellaneous	Time Table.		
Miscellaneous	Appendix "A". Lorries.		
Miscellaneous	1st Guards Brigade Platoon Competition.		
Operation(al) Order(s)	1st Guards Brigade Order No. 122	07/05/1917	07/05/1917
Miscellaneous	March Table.		
Miscellaneous	Warning Order.	15/05/1917	15/05/1917
Operation(al) Order(s)	1st Guards Brigade Order No. 123	18/05/1917	28/05/1917
Miscellaneous	March Table.		
Miscellaneous	Distribution Of 1st Guards Brigade On May 21st.	21/05/1917	21/05/1917
Miscellaneous	G.No. 2697/12/G.	04/05/1917	04/05/1917
Miscellaneous	Fourth Army No. G.S. 695.	20/05/1917	20/05/1917
Miscellaneous	Notes in Fire Control.		
Operation(al) Order(s)	1st Guards Brigade Order No. 124	28/05/1917	28/05/1917
Miscellaneous	Time Table.		
Miscellaneous	Appendix "A" Lorries.		

WO 95
12:3
May 1917

WAR DIARY or INTELLIGENCE SUMMARY

Army Form C. 2118
May, 1917
Hdqrs 1st Guards Brigade
Vol 22

Place	Date	Hour	Summary of Events and Information	Remarks and references to Appendices
BRONFAY FARM Camp 15.	May 1st		2nd Coldstream & 1st Irish Gds moved from MAUREPAS to ETRICOURT where they were encamped. These two Bns on Tuesday 2nd started work on the ROCQUIGNY-YTRES railway under the direction of 295th Coy R.E.	
	May 2nd		Final round of platoon competition carried out. The tactical exercise was disappointing in the show made by the platoon - Platoon commanders did not make a definite enough plan & did not seem to realise that the real use of any barrage was to enable assaulting troops to get within assaulting distance of them in offensive. The result of the competition is shown in appendix 357.	App 357
	May 3rd to May 5		Company training by 2nd Gren Gds & 3rd Cold Gds continued. As in platoon training great emphasis was laid on practising some form of open warfare & in the coy training more & more things it became apparent how deep rooted in the minds of platoon & coy commanders was the idea of trench to trench attacks - stereotyped formations - names fronts - execution of every movement under a creeping barrage	

WAR DIARY or INTELLIGENCE SUMMARY

Army Form C. 2118

(Erase heading not required.)

Place	Date	Hour	Summary of Events and Information	Remarks and references to Appendices
BRONFAY FM. Camp 15	May 3rd to 6th		Both flanks our own & from the enemy's artillery. 2nd Coys & 1st Field Coys continued work on FINS - ROCQUIGNY railway	appx 3.5.0
	May 7th		1st Field Coy Bde Order No 122 issued.	
	May 8th		3rd Coldstream Coys moved to LE TRANSLOY	
	May 9th		2nd Gren Coys moved to LES BOEUFS. 1st Fd Bde M.G. Coy did not move as previously ordered owing to a small number of casualties thereto.	
BRONFAY FM. to LE MESNIL-EN- ACRUBAISE	May 10th		Bde. H.Q. moved at 10 a.m.	
	May 11th		3rd Coldstream Coys moved from LE TRANSLOY to ROCQUIGNY taking over from 1st Bn. Scots Fds for work on ROCQUIGNY - FINS railway. Bde No P Coy moved to CHELU 2nd Bn. Gren Fds moved from LES BOEUFS to LE MESNIL taking over from 3rd Bn. Gren Fds for work on ROCQUIGNY - FINS railway.	
	May 12th		All Bns were now very comfortable in camps in a comparatively & clean area. Only a minimum number of N.C.O's & one officer per coy were went to work	

WAR DIARY or INTELLIGENCE SUMMARY

Army Form C. 2118

Place	Date	Hour	Summary of Events and Information	Remarks and references to Appendices
LE MESNIL EN-ARROUAISE	May 12th to May 14th		Daily on the railway. The remainder were kept back + trained daily on schemes under Bn. arrangements. Two Bde schemes for C.O.'s & adjutants were also held. Bn. courses for training of musketry instructors were held under Bn. arrangements. A Bde bombing course was held as well as a Bayonet fighting course for the advanced training of two N.C.O.'s (selected) per Bn. Jnr first class instructors. Information received from Div that Bde was to move into the CORBIE area ---	Aff. 359 Aff. 360
	May 15th		1st Bde Bde order No 123 issued. ---	
	May 18th		Bde moved as per Order No 123 (Aff 362). 2nd Bn. Bgn 2ℎ to BRONFAY Camp 15. 2nd Bn. Cdts 2ℎ. GURLU. 3rd Bn. lchs 2ℎ. BRONFAY Camp 15. Lnch 2ℎ CURLU. The day was a hot one but in spite of the fact that troops had recently done very little marching, the march was well carried out	
LE MESNIL to BRONFAY Camp 15.	May 20th			
BRONFAY Camp 15 to SAILLY MORETTE	May 21st		Bde H.Q. moved to SAILLY-LE-SEC LAURETTE instead of MORLANCOURT as originally arranged as the accommodation was better & less cramped. The day was not quite so hot & troops marched very well indeed - as per PM out. For distribution of Bde see last page of Aff. 360.	

Place	Date	Hour	Summary of Events and Information	Remarks and references to Appendices
SAILLY LABOURSE	May 22nd	10 am	Lecture by B.Gen. Sir Ivor Maxse to commanding officers on battle of Arras	
	May 22nd to May 29th		Owing to the amount of cultivation in the area little training beyond drill musketry & route marching could be done by troops themselves. One trench to trench attack scheme was carried out by Bde. H.Q. Officers affiliated to each practice. The h. coys company in the Bde. coys appeared to lack practice. The most noticeable faults were — Lack of organisation in assembly platoons & sections — This requires careful forethought which in most cases it did not receive — Leading waves apt to get too close to barrage — rear waves apt to let barrage get too far ahead — (this is the danger of creeping barrage) suffered up did not understand their duties. All coy commanders did own outpost & advance post scheme set by Bde H.Q. but this carried out to under B?. arrangements	Apps 362
	May 30th & 31st		10th Bde Order No 724 issued The Bde group moved by train in accordance with App 362 to the area round	

WAR DIARY
INTELLIGENCE SUMMARY
(Erase heading not required.)

Army Form C. 2118

Place	Date	Hour	Summary of Events and Information	Remarks and references to Appendices
RENESCURE.	May 30. & 31st		RENESCURE - PAS DE CALAIS. The journey was well & comfortably carried out, each train taking on an average 12 hours or running up to time. The route followed was AMIENS - ABBEVILLE - ETAPLES - BOULOGNE - CALAIS - ST OMER	
	31st	4 am	Bde H.Q. were established in RENESCURE.	

J.A. Jeffreys
Brig. General -
Commanding 1st Guards Bde

1st Guards Brigade Platoon Compotition.

Unit	Musketry	Bayonet Fighting	Drill & Turn out	Tactics	Total
	Possible 50.	Possible 48.	Possible 50.	Possible 60.	208.
2/Gren.Gds.	15.8	25.3	37.0	50.0	128.1
2/Cold.Gds.	12.0	20.8	36.0	34.0	102.8
3/Cold.Gds.	14.0	22.5	36.5	32.5	105.5
1/Irish Gds.	13.1	24.1	36.0	45.0	118.2

SECRET.

1st Guards Brigade Order No. 137.

Ref. Map - ALBERT 1/40,000.   May 7th, 1917.

1. (a) Movements will be carried out on May 8th, 9th and 10th
         in accordance with attached March Table.

    (b) All movement will be by Coy's. in fours at 500 yards
         interval and a similar interval will be left between
         every 4 transport vehicles.

    (c) Attention is called to this Office No.377 of 16th April
         1917 concerning March Discipline of Details and Transport.

2.   1st Line Transport will move with Units.

3.   Billeting parties will be sent in advance to take over
    Camps. Parties will be at the Camps to be taken over by 9 a.m.
    on the day their Unit moves.

4.   2nd Bn. Grenadier Guards and 3rd Bn. Coldstream Guards
    will work under Orders of 76th Field Coy., R.E. starting work
    on May 10th and 9th respectively.

         2nd Bn. Grenadier Guards and 3rd Bn. Coldstream Guards
    will send an Officer to report at H.Q., 76th Field Coy., R.E.
    at LES BOEUFS on May 9th and 8th respectively to find out
    details of work.

         1st Guards Brigade Machine Gun Company and Trench Mortar
    Battery will not be required for work at present.

5.   Orders as to relief of the two Guns found by 1st Guards
    Brigade Machine Gun Company at the PLATEAU will be issued later.

6.   Brigade H.Q., will close at BRONFAY and open at LE MESNIL
    at 10 a.m. on May 10th.

                ACKNOWLEDGE.
                                                    Captain,
                                    Brigade Major, 1st Guards Brigade.

Issued at 4-30 p.m.

Copy No.1 2nd Bn. Grenadier Guards.   Copy No.9 76th Field Coy., R.E.
        2 2nd Bn. Coldstream Guards.   10 Camp Commdt., BRONFAY.
        3 3rd Bn. Coldstream Guards.   11   "   "   CURLU.
        4 1st Bn. Irish Guards.   12 Supply Officer.
        5 Bde. Machine Gun Company.   13 Staff Captain.
        6 Bde. Trench Mortar Battery.   14 Signals.
        7 Guards Division, "G".   15 - 18 Retained.
        8 Guards Division, "Q".
        8 2nd Guards Brigade.

MARCH TABLE.

Date.	Unit.	From.	To.	Taking over from.	Route.	Remarks.
May 8th	3/Cold.Gds.	BRONFAY 16.	LE TRANSLOY.	1/Cold.Gds.	RICOURT-ILLEMONT-GINCHY.	(a) Not to arrive at LE TRANSLOY before 12-30 p.m. (b) Two lorries will be at BRONFAY Farm at 9 a.m.
9th	2/Gren.Gds.	BRONFAY 108.	LES BOEUFS.	2/Irish Gds.	-do-	(a) Not to arrive at LES BOEUFS before 12-30 p.m. (b) 2 lorries will be asked for.
	1st Gds.Bde. H.G.Coy. & T.M.Battery.	BRONFAY 16.	CURLU.	-	-do-	(a) Not to move before 2 p.m. Billeting party to report to Area Commdt., CURLU who will allot accommodation. (b) 1 wagon from Brigade H.Q., will be allotted to T.M.Battery.
10th	1st Gds.Bde. Headquarters.	BRONFAY 15.	LE MESNIL.	2nd Gds.Bde. Headquarters.	-do-	

SECRET.   1st G.B. No.789

            2nd Bn. Grenadier Guards.
            2nd Bn. Coldstream Guards.
            3rd Bn. Coldstream Guards.
            1st Bn. Irish Guards.
            Bde. Machine Gun Company.
            Bde. Trench Mortar Battery.
            No. 3 Coy. Guards Divnl. Train.
            Bde. Transport Officer.
            O.C., Signals.
            Staff Captain.

                            WARNING ORDER.

1.   The Brigade will move to the MORLANCOURT Area

    probably as follows :-

    May 17th.   1st Guards Bde. Machine Gun Company and Trench

                Mortar Battery.to MORLANCOURT.

    May 20th.   Brigade H.Q.,   ) Present billets
                2nd Bn. Grenadier Gds.   )   to
                3rd Bn. Coldstream Gds.)   BILLON.

                2nd Bn. Coldstream Gds.) Present billets
                1st Bn. Irish Gds.   )   to CLERY.

    May 21st.   Brigade H.Q.,   ) BILLON to MORLANCOURT.
                2nd Bn. Grenadier Gds.   ) BILLON to SAILLY LE SEC
                3rd Bn. Coldstream Gds.) and VAUX Sur SOMME.

                2nd Bn. Coldstream Gds.) MORLANCOURT.
                1st Bn. Irish Gds.   )

2.   Details of moves, billets and extra transport will

    be issued later.

                                              [signature]
                                                    Captain,
    15th May 1917.   Brigade Major, 1st Guards Brigade.

S E C R E T.

Copy No. 26

1st Guards Brigade Order No.123.

Ref. Maps - ALBERT. 1/40,000.
57 C. 1/40,000.   May 18th, 1917.

1. (a)   Movements will be carried out on May 20th and 21st in accordance with attached March Table.

    (b)   All movement will be by Coy's. in fours at 500 yards distance. A similar distance will be left between every 4 transport vehicles.

    (c)   After 3 hours marching on both May 20th and 21st, unless orders to the contrary on account of weather are received from these H.Q., there will be an hours halt during which dinners or a haversack ration will be consumed. Units will be careful that distances are maintained on moving off again.

    (d)   Except for para 1 (c), the usual halts will be made i.e. from 0.50 to the hour.

2. (a)   1st Line Transport will move with Units.

    (b)   One lorry per Battalion is available for move each day. This lorry can do two journeys if necessary. Time of arrival of lorry each day will be notified later direct to Units.

3.   Billeting parties will report at 11 a.m. on the date on which their Unit moves, to the Camp Commandant or Town Major of the billets to be taken over.

4. (a)   Unless orders to contrary are received by 5 a.m. on May 20th, all tents in the Camps at present occupied by Battalions will be struck and collected on the nearest roadway accessible to lorries. The site of proposed dump will be wired to this Office by Units as soon as possible.

    (b)   A guard of 1 N.C.O. and 3 O.R. will be left on tents thus collected until they are picked up by lorries of XIV or XV Corps. These Guards will be rationed by nearest Town Majors or Area Commandants - arrangements for rations being made by Units direct.

    (c)   When tents have been collected Guards will rejoin their Units. Use can be made of empty Supply Trains from ROCQUIGNY.

5.   Work on Railways will cease after May 19th.

1.

(2)

6. (a) O.C., Signals will arrange for Brigade Signal Office to close at LE MESNIL at 10 a.m. on May 20th and open at BRONFAY at the same hour.

   (b) Similarly, on May 21st O.C., Signals will arrange to close at BRONFAY at 10 a.m. and open at MORLANCOURT at the same hour.

   ACKNOWLEDGE.

   Captain,
   Brigade Major, 1st Guards Brigade.

Issued at 2-30 p.m.

Copy No. 1 2nd Bn. Grenadier Guards.
       2 2nd Bn. Coldstream Guards.
       3 3rd Bn. Coldstream Guards.
       4 1st Bn. Irish Guards.
       5 Bde. Machine Gun Company.
       6 Bde. Trench Mortar Battery.
       7 Guards Division, "G".
       8 Guards Division, "Q".
       9 3rd Guards Brigade.
     10 O.C., Transport 1st Bn. Welsh Gds.
     11 55th Field Coy. R.E.
     12 No. 3 Coy. Guards Divnl. Train.
Copy No. 13 No. 4 Field Ambulance.
     14 Town Major, ETRICOURT.
     15 " " LE MESNIL.
     16 " " ROCQUIGNY.
     17 " " CURLU.
     18 " " BRONFAY.
     19 " " MORLANCOURT.
     20 " " SAILLY-LE-SEC.
     21 " " VAUX-Sur-SOMME.
     22 Bde. Transport Officer.
     23 O.C., Signals.
     24 Staff Captain.
     25 - 27 Retained.

MARCH TABLE.

Date.	Unit.	From.	To.	Route.	Starting Point.	Time.	Remarks.
May 20th.	3rd Bn. Coldstream Gds.	ROCQUIGNY.	BRONFAY Camp 15.	SAILLY SAILLISEL- COMBLES - MAUREPAS - MARICOURT.	Rd junct O.27.d.7.8.	8 a.m.	If fine, personnel may march across country to SAILLY - BAPAUME Rd but must not debouch onto it before 10 a.m.
	2nd Bn. Grenadier Gds.	LE MESNIL.	-do-	-do-	-do-	9 a.m.	
	Brigade H.Q.,	-do-	-do-	-do-	-do-	10 a.m.	
	1st Bn. Irish Gds.	ETRICOURT.	CURLU.	MOISLAINS - HAUT- ALLAINES - CLERY.	Cross rds V.13.c.6.5.	8 a.m.	
	2nd Bn. Coldstream Gds.	-do-	-do-	-do-	-do-	9 a.m.	
	85th Field Coy. R.E.	-do-	-do-	-do-	-do-	10 a.m.	
21st.	3rd Bn. Coldstream Gds.	BRONFAY Camp 15.	VAUX-SUR-SOMME.	Rd junct L.15.b.3.8 - L.15.a. - cross rds L.14.d.4.3 - L.13.c.con. - J.20.b.9.1.	Camp 108.	8 a.m.	
	2nd Bn. Grenadier Gds.	-do-	SAILLY-LE-SEC.	as for 3/C.G. to cross rds J.18.c. 9.2. thence to SAILLY-LE-SEC.	-do-	8-45 a.m.	
	Brigade H.Q.,	-do-	MORLAN- COURT.	as for 3/C.G. to cross rds K.21.b. 9.9 thence to MORLANCOURT.	-do-	9-30 a.m.	
	No.4 Field Ambulance.	MARICOURT.	-do-	-do-	Rd junct A.21.a.2.9.	9-15 a.m.	

(2)

Date.	Unit.	From.	To.	Route.	Starting Point.	Time.	Remarks.
May 21st.	2nd Bn. Coldstream Gds.	CUPLU.	MORLANCOURT.	MARICOURT-BRONFAY FARM-Rd junct L.15.b.5.8 - L.15.a. - cross rds L.14.d.4.8 - L.13.cen. - cross rds K.21.b.9.9.	Cross rds A.30.b.8.5.	8-45 a.m.	
	1st Bn. Irish Gds.	—do—	—do—	—do—	—do—	9-30 a.m.	
	55th Field Coy. R.E.	—do—	CORBIE Area.	as for 2/C.G. to K.21.b.9.9. thence along main CORBIE Road to CORBIE.	—do—	10-15 a.m.	
	Transport, 1st Bn. Welsh Gds.	—do—	—do—	—do—	—do—	10-45 a.m.	

Distribution of 1st Guards Brigade on May 21st.

Brigade H.Q., ...	MORLANCOURT.
2nd Bn. Grenadier Guards	SAILLY-LE-SEC.
2nd Bn. Coldstream Guards	MORLANCOURT.
3rd Bn. Coldstream Guards	VAUX-sur-SOMME.
1st Bn. Irish Guards	MORLANCOURT.
Machine Gun Company	-do-
Trench Mortar Battery	-do-
75th Field Coy. R.E.	SAILLY-LE-SEC.
No.4 Field Ambulance	MORLANCOURT.
No.3 Coy. Guards Divnl. Train	-do-

SECRET.   Copy No. 18

1st Guards Brigade Order No. 124.

Ref. Maps — AMIENS & HAZEBROUCK
Sheets 1/100,000.   May 28th, 1917.

1. (a) On May 30th and 31st the Brigade will entrain in accordance with attached Time Table.

   (b) On arrival in new area 1st Guards Brigade Group will be billeted in RENESCURE Area.

   (c) Allotment of billets in detail and routes thither from Detraining Stations will be notified to O.C., each Train on arrival at Detraining Station.

2. Entraining Station will be EDGEHILL (DERNACOURT).

   Detraining Station will be CASSEL.

3. (a) Transport, with loading parties (1 Officer 50 O.R.) will be at the Entraining Station 3 hours before the departure of the Train and will report to the R.T.O. on arrival.

   (b) Personnel will arrive at the Entraining Station one hour before the hour of departure of each Train.

4. Baggage and Supply Wagons will accompany Units.

5. (a) All billeting parties of the Brigade will travel on the first Train.

   (b) Billeting parties will consist of :-

       1 Officer   )
       4 Other Ranks   ) .... per Battalion.   } with
                                                              } bicycle
       1 Other Rank   .... for all other Units

6. (a) Troops entraining up to 12 midnight on 30th inst., will carry rations for the 31st inst.
   These troops will not refill on the 30th inst.,
   Rations for the 1st prox., will be drawn on 31st inst., on arrival in new area, by Supply Wagons, on main CASSEL - ARQUES Road immediately East of the level crossing at PONT ROUGE. (Sheet HAZEBROUCK 5a. 1/100,000.)

   (b) Troops entraining after midnight on 30th inst. will carry rations for the 31st and 1st; rations for the 1st being drawn at Entraining Stations before entrainment. Ordinary refilling will not take place for these troops on the 30th inst.,

7. Units having Detachments travelling by separate Train will wire at once to S.S.O., repeated Guards Division, "Q", and 1st Guards Brigade, the exact ration strength of men and horses contained in each Train.
   These figures will, under no circumstances, be changed.

8. (a) One lorry per Unit is available to move extra baggage to Entraining Station. For details see APPENDIX "A".

   (b) The Guards Divnl. Supply Column will be responsible for the transport of the surplus baggage of Units, from the Detraining Stations, to their respective billets.

9. Brigade H.Q., will close at SAILLY LAURETTE at 7 a.m. on 30th inst and re-open at RENESCURE on arrival.

ACKNOWLEDGE.

Captain,
Brigade Major, 1st Guards Brigade.

Issued at 2 pm

No. 1 2nd Bn. Grenadier Guards.
2 2nd Bn. Coldstream Guards.
3 3rd Bn. Coldstream Guards.
4 1st Bn. Irish Guards.
5 Bde. Machine Gun Company.
6 Bde. Trench Mortar Battery.
7 75th Field Coy. R.E.
8 No.3 Coy. Divnl. Train.

No. 9 No. 4 Field Ambulance.
10 Guards Division, "G".
11 Guards Division, "Q".
12 2nd Guards Brigade.
13 R.T.O., EDGEHILL.
14 Town Major, SAILLY LAURETTE.
15 O.C. Signals.
16. Staff Captain.
17-19. Retained.

TIME TABLE.
****

Date.	Unit.	Route to Entraining Station.	Starting Point and Time.	Approx. time of departure.	Approx. time of arrival.	Date.
May 30th	Brigade H.Q.,	MORLANCOURT – MEAULTE.	SAILLY LAURETTE Church. 8 a.m.	11.16.	23.16.	30th
"	1/Coy. 1 Cooker. 2/Cold.Gds.	–do–	Rd. junct. 200 yds. East of V of VILLERS. 9 a.m.	8.30 –do–	–do–	–do–
"	1st Gds.Bde. M.G.Company.	–do–	–do– at 9.15 am.	8.45 –do–	–do–	–do–
"	1st Gds.Bde. T.M.Battery.	–do–	–do– at 9–15 am.	–do–	–do–	–do–
"	2/Cold.Gds. less 1 Coy. & 1 Cooker.	–do–	As desired.	15.06.	3.06.	31st.
"	1/Irish Gds. less 1 Coy. & 1 Cooker.	–do–	–do–	19.56.	7.56.	–do–

2.

P.T.O.

(2)

Date.	Unit.	Route to Entraining Station.	Starting Point and Time.	Approx. time of departure.	Approx. time of arrival.	Date.
May 30th	2/Gren.Gds. less 1 Coy. & 1 Cooker.	TREUX – BUIRE.	As desired.	23.06.	11.06.	31st
31st	3/Cold.Gds. less 1 Coy. & Cooker.	MERICOURT – TREUX – BUIRE.	—do—	3.06.	15.06.	31st
"	1 Coy. 1 Cooker 1/Irish Gds.	MEAULTE.	—do—	15.06.	3.06.	1st
"	No.3 Coy. Divnl. Train.	MEAULTE.	—do—	15.06.	3.06.	1st
"	75th Field Coy. R.E.	TREUX – BUIRE.	—do—	15.06.	3.06.	1st
"	1 Coy. & Cooker 2/Gren.Gds.	TREUX – BUIRE.	—do—	19.56.	7.56.	1st No.4 Fld.Amb. will also travel on this train.
"	1 Coy. & Cooker 3/Cold.Gds.	MERICOURT – TREUX – BUIRE.	—do—	19.56.	7.56.	—do—

Troops of 1st Guards Brigade will give way to troops of 2nd Guards Brigade if met on the road to Entraining Station.

APPENDIX "A".

LORRIES.

	Rendezvous.	Time.	Destination.	Return & report to.	Time.
Lorry No.1.	Brigade H.Q., SAILLY LAURETTE.	6 a.m. 30th.	EDGEHILL.	2/Cold.Gds. MORLANCOURT.	10 am.
Lorry No.2.	M.G.Company. MORLANCOURT.	7 a.m.	EDGEHILL.	1/Irish Gds. MORLANCOURT.	12 noon.
Lorry No.3.	T.M.Battery.	7 a.m.	EDGEHILL.	2/Gren.Gds. SAILLY-LE-Sec.	12 noon.
Lorry No.1.	2/Cold.Gds. MORLANCOURT.	10 a.m.	EDGEHILL.	3/Cold.Gds. VAUX-SUR-SOMME.	4 pm.
Lorry No.2.	1/Irish Gds. MORLANCOURT.	12 noon.	EDGEHILL.		
Lorry No.3.	2/Gren.Gds. SAILLY-LE-Sec.	12 noon.	EDGEHILL.		
Lorry No.1.	3/Cold.Gds. VAUX-SUR-SOMME.	4 p.m.	EDGEHILL.		

No.1 Lorry for Bde. H.Q.,)
No.2 Lorry for M.G.Coy.) Will do <u>one</u> journey.
No.3 Lorry for T.M.Bty.)

Lorry for Battalions will do two journeys if required.

1st Guards Brigade Platoon Competition.

Unit	Musketry	Bayonet Fighting	Drill & Turn out	Tactics	Total
	Possible 50.	Possible 48.	Possible 50.	Possible 60.	208.
2/Gren.Gds.	15.8	25.3	37.0	50.0	128.1
2/Cold.Gds.	12.0	20.78	36.0	34.0	102.8
3/Cold.Gds.	14.0	22.45	36.5	32.5	105.5
1/Irish Gds.	13.1	24.1	36.0	45.0	118.2

SECRET.   Copy No. 15

1st Guards Brigade Order No. 122.

Ref. Map - ALBERT 1/40,000.   May 7th, 1917.

1. (a) Movements will be carried out on May 8th, 9th and 10th in accordance with attached March Table.

    (b) All movement will be by Coy's. in fours at 500 yards interval and a similar interval will be left between every 4 transport vehicles.

    (c) Attention is called to this Office No.377 of 16th April 1917 concerning March Discipline of Details and Transport.

2. 1st Line Transport will move with Units.

3. Billeting parties will be sent in advance to take over Camps. Parties will be at the Camps to be taken over by 9 a.m. on the day their Unit moves.

4. 2nd Bn. Grenadier Guards and 3rd Bn. Coldstream Guards will work under Orders of 76th Field Coy., R.E. starting work on May 10th and 9th respectively.

    2nd Bn. Grenadier Guards and 3rd Bn. Coldstream Guards will send an Officer to report at H.Q., 76th Field Coy., R.E. at LES BOEUFS on May 9th and 8th respectively to find out details of work.

    1st Guards Brigade Machine Gun Company and Trench Mortar Battery will not be required for work at present.

5. Orders as to relief of the two Guns found by 1st Guards Brigade Machine Gun Company at the PLATEAU will be issued later.

6. Brigade H.Q., will close at BRONFAY and open at LE MESNIL at 10 a.m. on May 10th.

ACKNOWLEDGE.
                                                          Captain,
                                        Brigade Major, 1st Guards Brigade.

Issued at 4.30 pm

Copy No.1 2nd Bn. Grenadier Guards.   Copy No.9 76th Field Coy., R.E.
        2 2nd Bn. Coldstream Guards.   10 Camp Commdt., BRONFAY.
        3 3rd Bn. Coldstream Guards.   11   "   "   CURLU.
        4 1st Bn. Irish Guards.   12 Supply Officer.
        5 Bde. Machine Gun Company.   13 Staff Captain.
        6 Bde. Trench Mortar Battery.   14 Signals.
        7 Guards Division, "G".   -15 - 18 Retained.
        8 Guards Division, "Q".
       *8 2nd Guards Brigade.

MARCH TABLE.
****

Date.	Unit.	From.	To.	Taking over from.	Route.	Remarks.
May 8th	3/Cold.Gds.	BRONFAY 13.	LE TRANSLOY.	1/Cold.Gds.	RICOURT–ILLEMONT–GINCHY.	(a) Not to arrive at LE TRANSLOY before 12-30 p.m. (b) Two lorries will be at BRONFAY Farm at 9 a.m.
9th	2/Gren.Gds.	BRONFAY 108.	LES BOEUFS.	2/Irish Gds.	-do-	(a) Not to arrive at LES BOEUFS before 12-30 p.m. (b) 2 lorries will be asked for.
	1st Gds.Bde. M.G.Coy. & T.M.Battery.	BRONFAY 16.	CURLU.	-	-do-	(a) Not to move before 2 p.m. Billeting party to report to Area Commdt., CURLU who will allot accommodation. (b) 1 wagon from Brigade H.Q., will be allotted to T.M.Battery.
10th	1st Gds.Bde. Headquarters.	BRONFAY 15.	LE MESNIL.	2nd Gds.Bde. Headquarters.	-do-	

SECRET.   1st G.B. No.789.

2nd Bn. Grenadier Guards.
2nd Bn. Coldstream Guards.
3rd Bn. Coldstream Guards.
1st Bn. Irish Guards.
Bde. Machine Gun Company.
Bde. Trench Mortar Battery.
No. 3 Coy. Guards Divnl. Train.
Bde. Transport Officer.
O.C., Signals.
Staff Captain.

WARNING ORDER.

1.   The Brigade will move to the MORLANCOURT Area probably as follows :-

   May 17th.   1st Guards Bde. Machine Gun Company and Trench Mortar Battery to MORLANCOURT.

   May 20th.   Brigade H.Q.,   ) Present billets
                     2nd Bn. Grenadier Gds.)   to
                     3rd Bn. Coldstream Gds.)   BILLON.

                2nd Bn. Coldstream Gds.) Present billets
                1st Bn. Irish Gds.   ) to CLERY.

   May 21st.   Brigade H.Q.,   ) BILLON to MORLANCOURT.
                2nd Bn. Grenadier Gds.) BILLON to SAILLY LE SEC
                3rd Bn. Coldstream Gds.) and VAUX Sur SOMME.

                2nd Bn. Coldstream Gds.)
                1st Bn. Irish Gds.   ) MORLANCOURT.

2.   Details of moves, billets and extra transport will be issued later.

W B Smith
                                                            Captain,
15th May 1917.   Brigade Major, 1st Guards Brigade.

SECRET.

Copy No. 25

1st Guards Brigade Order No.123.
****

Ref. Maps - ALBERT. 1/40,000.
57 C. 1/40,000.

May 18th, 1917.

1. (a) Movements will be carried out on May 20th and 21st in accordance with attached March Table.

   (b) All movement will be by Coy's. in fours at 500 yards distance. A similar distance will be left between every 4 transport vehicles.

   (c) After 3 hours marching on both May 20th and 21st, unless orders to the contrary on account of weather are received from these H.Q., there will be an hours halt during which dinners or a haversack ration will be consumed. Units will be careful that distances are maintained on moving off again.

   (d) Except for para 1 (c), the usual halts will be made i.e. from 0.50 to the hour.

2. (a) 1st Line Transport will move with Units.

   (b) One lorry per Battalion is available for move each day. This lorry can do two journeys if necessary. Time of arrival of lorry each day will be notified later direct to Units.

3. Billeting parties will report at 11 a.m. on the date on which their Unit moves, to the Camp Commandant or Town Major of the billets to be taken over.

4. (a) Unless orders to contrary are received by 5 a.m. on May 20th, all tents in the Camps at present occupied by Battalions will be struck and collected on the nearest roadway accessible to lorries. The site of proposed dump will be wired to this Office by Units as soon as possible.

   (b) A guard of 1 N.C.O. and 3 O.R. will be left on tents thus collected until they are picked up by lorries of XIV or XV Corps. These Guards will be rationed by nearest Town Majors or Area Commandants - arrangements for rations being made by Units direct.

   (c) When tents have been collected Guards will rejoin their Units. Use can be made of empty Supply Trains from ROCQUIGNY.

5. Work on Railways will cease after May 19th.

1.

(2)

6. (a) O.C., Signals will arrange for Brigade Signal Office to close at LE MESNIL at 10 a.m. on May 20th and open at BRONFAY at the same hour.

   (b) Similarly, on may 21st O.C., Signals will arrange to close at BRONFAY at 10 a.m. and open at MORLANCOURT at the same hour.

ACKNOWLEDGE.

Captain,
Brigade Major, 1st Guards Brigade.

Issued at 2-30 p.m.

Copy No.1 2nd Bn. Grenadier Guards.	Copy No.13 No.4 Field Ambulance.
2 2nd Bn. Coldstream Guards.	14 Town Major, ETRICOURT.
3 3rd Bn. Coldstream Guards.	15 " " LE MESNIL.
4 1st Bn. Irish Guards.	16 " " ROCQUIGNY.
5 Bde. Machine Gun Company.	17 " " CURLU.
6 Bde. Trench Mortar Battery.	18 " " BRONFAY.
7 Guards Division, "G".	19 " " MORLANCOURT.
8 Guards Division, "Q".	20 " " SAILLY-LE-SEC.
9 3rd Guards Brigade.	21 " " VAUX-Sur-SOMME.
10 O.C., Transport 1st Bn. Welsh Gds.	22 Bde. Transport Officer.
11 55th Field Coy. R.E.	23 O.C., Signals.
12 No.3 Coy. Guards Divnl. Train.	24 Staff Captain.
	25 - 27 Retained.

MARCH TABLE.

Date.	Unit.	From.	To.	Route.	Starting Point.	Time.	Remarks.
May 20th.	3rd Bn. Coldstream Gds.	ROCQUIGNY.	BRONFAY Camp 15.	SAILLY SAILLISEL - COMBLES - HARDECOURT - MARICOURT.	Rd junct O.27.d.7.8.	8 a.m.	
	2nd Bn. Grenadier Gds.	LE MESNIL.	-do-	-do-	-do-	9 a.m.	If fine, personnel may march across country to SAILLY - BAPAUME Rd but must not debouch onto it before 10 a.m.
	Brigade H.Q.,	-do-	-do-	-do-	-do-	10 a.m.	
	1st Bn. Irish Gds.	ETRICOURT.	CURLU.	MOISLAINS - HAUT ALLAINES - CLERY.	Cross rds V.13.c.6.5.	8 a.m.	
	2nd Bn. Coldstream Gds.	-do-	-do-	-do-	-do-	9 a.m.	
	25th Field Coy. R.E.	-do-	-do-	-do-	-do-	10 a.m.	
21st.	3rd Bn. Coldstream Gds.	BRONFAY Camp 15.	VAUX-SUR-SOMME.	Rd junct L.15.b.3.8 - L.15.a. - cross rds L.14.d.4.3 - L.13.cen. - J.20.b.9.1.	Camp 108.	8 a.m.	
	2nd Bn. Grenadier Gds.	-do-	SAILLY-LE-SEC.	as for 3/C.G. to cross rds J.18.c. 9.2. thence to SAILLY-LE-SEC.	-do-	8-45 a.m.	
	Erigade H.Q.,	-do-	MORLAN-COURT.	as for 3/C.G. to cross rds K.21.b. 9.9 thence to MORLANCOURT.	-do-	9-30 a.m.	
	No.4 Field Ambulance.	MARICOURT.	-do-	-do-	Rd junct A.21.a.2.9.	9-15 a.m.	

(2)

Date.	Unit.	From.	To.	Route.	Starting Point.	Time.	Remarks.
May 21st.	2nd Bn. Coldstream Gds.	CURLU.	MORLANCOURT.	MARICOURT-BRONFAY FARM-Rd junct L.15. A.30.b.8.5. b.5.8 - L.15.a. - cross rds L.14.d.4.8 - L.13.cen. - cross rds K.21.b.9.9.	Cross rds A.30.b.8.5.	8-45 a.m.	
	1st Bn. Irish Gds.	-do-	-do-	-do-	-do-	9-30 a.m.	
	55th Field Coy. R.E.	-do-	CORBIE Area.	as for 2/C.G. to K.21.b.9.9. thence along main CORBIE Road to CORBIE.	-do-	10-15 a.m.	
	Transport, 1st Bn. Welsh Gds.	-do-	-do-	-do-	-do-	10-45 a.m.	

Distribution of 1st Guards Brigade on May 21st.

Brigade H.Q.,	~~MORLANCOURT~~ SAILLY LORETTE
2nd Bn. Grenadier Guards	SAILLY-LE-SEC.
2nd Bn. Coldstream Guards	MORLANCOURT.
3rd Bn. Coldstream Guards	VAUX-sur-SOMME.
1st Bn. Irish Guards	MORLANCOURT.
Machine Gun Company	-do-
Trench Mortar Battery	-do-
75th Field Coy. R.E.	SAILLY-LE-SEC.
No.4 Field Ambulance	MORLANCOURT.
No.3 Coy. Guards Divnl. Train	-do-

G.D.No. 2697/12/G.

C.R.E.
1st Guards Brigade.
2nd Guards Brigade.
3rd Guards Brigade.
Pioneer Battalion.
Works Battalion.

The Commander in Chief sent for me to-day and expressed in the most flattering terms his gratification at the manner in which all ranks of the Guards Division have worked in pushing forward Roads and Railways.

The General Officer Commanding the Army also expressed his great pleasure at what had been done.

I wish all ranks to hear that their good work has been noticed.

I am very pleased to record the fact that the usual high standard of the Guards Division has been maintained, not only in billets and in trenches, but also when employed on work behind the lines.

In this way a fitting example has been set of what a Division should be.

G. Fielding

4th April 1917.

Major General,
Commanding Guards Division.

Fourth Army No. G.S.695.

Guards Division.

      It is now nine months since the Division joined the Fourth Army, and I cannot allow them to leave without expressing my thanks for the excellent services they have performed, and the high example they have set at all times to the Army in general. Whether in battle, in holding and organising the line, or in work in the back areas, they have maintained that standard of discipline and fighting spirit which has always characterised Guardsmen, and of which all Guardsmen are justly proud. I have been particularly struck at the very excellent work they have done in connection with railway construction, and it is largely due to their labours that the Transportation Services in this area are now in such a satisfactory condition.

      It is a matter of much regret to me that the Division is now leaving the Fourth Army, and I shall look forward in the future to the time when it may be my good fortune to again find them under my command.

H.Q., Fourth Army,
20th May, 1917.

Rawlinson

General,
Commanding Fourth Army.

SECRET.   Copy No. 17

1st Guards Brigade Order No. 124.

Ref. Maps - AMIENS & HAZEBROUCK
Sheets 1/100,000.   May 28th, 1917.

1. (a) On May 30th and 31st the Brigade will entrain in
         accordance with attached Time Table.

    (b) On arrival in new area 1st Guards Brigade Group will
         be billeted in RENESCURE Area.

    (c) Allotment of billets in detail and routes thither from
         Detraining Stations will be notified to O.C., each
         Train on arrival at Detraining Station.

2.   Entraining Station will be EDGEHILL (DERNACOURT).

         Detraining Station will be CASSEL.

3. (a) Transport, with loading parties (1 Officer 50 O.R.)
         will be at the Entraining Station 3 hours before the
         departure of the Train and will report to the R.T.O.
         on arrival.

    (b) Personnel will arrive at the Entraining Station one hour
         before the hour of departure of each Train.

4.   Baggage and Supply Wagons will accompany Units.

5. (a) All billeting parties of the Brigade will travel on the
         first Train.

    (b) Billeting parties will consist of :-

             1 Officer   )
             4 Other Ranks) .... per Battalion.   } with
                                                               } bicycle
             1 Other Rank   .... for all other Units.

6. (a) Troops entraining up to 12 midnight on 30th inst., will
         carry rations for the 31st inst.,
         These troops will not refil on the 30th inst.,
         Rations for the 1st prox., will be drawn on 31st inst.,
         on arrival in new area, by Supply Wagons, on main
         CASSEL - ARQUES Road immediately East of the level
         crossing at FORT ROUGE. (Sheet HAZEBROUCK 5A, 1/100,000.)

    (b) Troops entraining after midnight on 30th inst., will
         carry rations for the 31st and 1st; rations for the
         1st being drawn at Entraining Stations before entrainment.
         Ordinary refilling will not take place for these troops
         on the 30th inst.,

7.   Units having Detachments travelling by separate Train
    will wire at once to S.S.O., repeated Guards Division, "Q", and
    1st Guards Brigade, the exact ration strength of men and horses
    contained in each Train.
    These figures will, under no circumstances, be changed.

1.

P.T.O.

8. (a) One lorry per Unit is available to move extra baggage to Entraining Station. For details see APPENDIX "A".

    (b) The Guards Divnl. Supply Column will be responsible for the transport of the surplus baggage of Units, from the Detraining Stations, to their respective billets.

9. Brigade H.Q., will close at SAILLY LAURETTE at 7 a.m. on 30th inst and re-open at RENESCURE on arrival.

ACKNOWLEDGE.

                                                Captain,
                      Brigade Major, 1st Guards Brigade.

Issued at 2 pmi

No.1 2nd Bn. Grenadier Guards.	No.9 No. 4 Field Ambulance.
2 2nd Bn. Coldstream Guards.	10 Guards Division, "G".
3 3rd Bn. Coldstream Guards.	11 Guards Division, "Q".
4 1st Bn. Irish Guards.	12 2nd Guards Brigade.
5 Bde. Machine Gun Company.	13 R.T.O., EDGEHILL.
6 Bde. Trench Mortar Battery.	14 Town Major, SAILLY LAURETTE.
7 75th Field Coy. R.E.	15 O.C. Signals.
8 No.3 Coy. Divnl. Train.	16. Staff Captain.
	17-19 Retained

TIME TABLE.

Date.	Unit.	Route to Entraining Station.	Starting Point and Time.	Approx. time of departure.	Approx. time of arrival.	Date.
May 30th	Brigade H.Q., 1 Coy. 1 Cooker. 2/Cold.Gds.	MORLANCOURT - MEAULTE.	SAILLY LAURETTE Church. 8 a.m.	11.16.	23.16.	30th
"	1 Coy. 1 Cooker. 2/Cold.Gds.	—do—	Rd. junct. 200 yds. East of V of VILLERS. 9 a.m.	—do—	—do—	—do—
"	1st Gds.Bde. M.G.Company.	—do—	—do— at 9.5 am.	—do—	—do—	—do—
"	1st Gds.Bde. T.M.Battery.	—do—	—do— at 9-15 am.	—do—	—do—	—do—
"	2/Cold.Gds. less 1 Coy. & 1 Cooker.	—do—	As desired.	15.06.	3.06.	31st.
"	1/Irish Gds. less 1 Coy. & 1 Cooker.	—do—	—do—	19.56.	7.56.	—do—

2.

P.T.O.

(2)

Date.	Unit.	Route to Entraining Station.	Starting Point and Time.	Approx. time of departure.	Approx. time of arrival.	Date.
May 30th	2/Gren.Gds. less 1 Coy. & 1 Cooker.	?EUX - BUIRE.	As desired.	23.06.	11.06.	31st
31st	3/Cold.Gds. less 1 Coy. & Cooker.	MERICOURT - TREUX - BUIRE.	—do—	3.06.	15.06.	31st
"	1 Coy. 1 Cooker 1/Irish Gds.	MEAULTE.	—do—	15.06.	3.06.	1st
"	No.3 Coy. Divnl. Train.	MEAULTE.	—do—	15.06.	3.06.	1st
"	75th Field Coy. R.E.	TREUX - BUIRE.	—do—	15.06.	3.06.	1st
"	1 Coy. & Cooker 2/Gren.Gds.	TREUX - BUIRE.	—do—	19.56.	7.56.	1st No.4 Fld.Amb. will also travel on this train.
"	1 Coy. & Cooker 3/Cold.Gds.	MERICOURT - TREUX - BUIRE.	—do—	19.56.	7.56.	—do—

Troops of 1st Guards Brigade will give way to troops of
2nd Guards Brigade if met on the road to Entraining Station.

APPENDIX "A".

LORRIES.

	Rendezvous.	Time.	Destination.	Return & report to.	Time.
Lorry No.1.	Brigade H.Q., SAILLY LAURETTE.	6 a.m. 30th.	EDGEHILL.	2/Cold.Gds. MORLANCOURT.	10 am.
Lorry No.2.	M.G.Company. MORLANCOURT.	7 a.m.	EDGEHILL.	1/Irish Gds. MORLANCOURT.	12 noon.
Lorry No.3.	T.M.Battery.	7 a.m.	EDGEHILL.	2/Gren.Gds. SAILLY-LE-Sec.	12 noon.
Lorry No.1.	2/Cold.Gds. MORLANCOURT.	10 a.m.	EDGEHILL.	3/Cold.Gds. VAUX-SUR-SOMME.	4 pm.
Lorry No.2.	1/Irish Gds. MORLANCOURT.	12 noon.	EDGEHILL.		
Lorry No.3.	2/Gren.Gds. SAILLY-LE-Sec.	12 noon.	EDGEHILL.		
Lorry No.1.	3/Cold.Gds. VAUX-SUR-SOMME.	4 p.m.	EDGEHILL.		

No.1 Lorry for Bde. H.Q.,)
No.2 Lorry for M.G.Coy.) Will do <u>one</u> journey.
No.3 Lorry for T.M.Bty.)

Lorry for Battalions will do two journeys if required.

www.ingramcontent.com/pod-product-compliance
Lightning Source LLC
Chambersburg PA
CBHW081500160426
43193CB00013B/2546